The ESSENTIAL PRINCIPLES of TAIJI QUAN

N.L. DEYE

Copyright © 2013 N.L. Deye

All rights reserved.

ISBN 10:148013449
ISBN 13:978-1480134447

DEDICATION

To my students with whom I share my understanding
of the great art of Taiji Quan

CONTENTS

	Acknowledgments	vii
1	Introduction	1
2	A Brief History	5
3	The Dao of Taiji Quan	11
4	The Power of Qi	15
5	The Ten Essential Principles	19
6	The Cardinal Principle	21
7	Mechanics	25
8	Movement	51
8	Mindfulness	71
10	The Development of Practice	95
	Resources	105

ACKNOWLEDGMENTS

It is with respect and honor that I bow deeply to my parents,
Norman and Marilyn Brue, for sharing their passion for life,
for nurturing this independent spirit with limitless love
and guidance, and for fostering the characteristics required
for lofty goals and adventurous journeys.

I am grateful for the opportunities and experiences that
have taken me around the world, introducing me to
teachers of all walks and ages.

I give thanks to all who have encouraged me
on this path of the Dao ~
my Taiji colleagues and friends; and, especially
my husband, Ross, who travels with me,
joining my spirit with love and light.

INTRODUCTION

There are five major styles of Taiji Quan, the ancient oriental system of gentle movements aimed at addressing the body and mind as an interconnected system. Forms have evolved within each of these individual styles through the elements of time, place, teacher style and student interpretation. Even today, from one school to another, variations exist within the same form. Movements can appear quite different at first glance. Initially, this can be disconcerting.

My initiation to Taiji began as a serious attempt to learn the Yang Style short form with a dedicated group in Ohio. After two years of conscientious study, imagine my surprise and confusion when I encountered a teacher from Seattle who performed quite different – yet similar - movements of the same form. I was catapulted into a new layer of study.

How could the choreography of each movement require such exactness yet allow for such variation within the same form? Rather than becoming preoccupied with the differences, I shifted my focus to finding the similarities. In an attempt to find some center ground of understanding, I reflected on the original Ten Essential Principles of Taiji, the tenets that promise successful practice for the player regardless of the form.

For the interested individual, media on Taiji Quan is readily available. However, the concentration rests either in a step-by-step approach to learning a form's choreography or in the esoteric, philosophical writings that require a more seasoned student. My search to find writings that emphasized and clearly described the original Ten Essential Principles taught by Grandmaster Yang Ch'eng-fu and published in 1925 proved fruitless.

Therefore, it is my goal to interpret and clarify the key principles that thread through Taiji's richness. It is my hope that with deeper understanding and renewed awareness, a transformation will be cultivated in the practice of all players willing to contemplate and incorporate those principles.

The Pinyin System of Spelling and Pronunciation

The Chinese language consists of pictures or ideograms rather than letters. This has made true interpretations of original writings difficult. Until recently, the Wade-Giles system was used to represent the sound of these ideograms. However, this system did not set an international standard and various countries around the world devised their own method of representing the language. Rather than clarifying interpretations, the inconsistencies in pronunciation and spelling made understanding more difficult.

To rectify this problem, in 1958, linguists from the People's Republic of China devised a standard phonetic system called Pinyin. This system was designed to represent the official Chinese pronunciation of characters using letters and is used in all translations published in China today. Gradually, the Western world has been adopting this system as the international standard. According to the Library of Congress website, the Pinyin system is the "standard used by the United Nations and most of the world's media." In efforts to accept and encourage the adoption, this writing will use the Pinyin system of spelling and pronunciation.

Standard Phonetic Systems

Pinyin	Wade-Giles	Pronunciation
Taiji	T'ai Chi	tie jee
Taiji Quan	T'ai Chi Ch'uan	tie jee chuan
Qi	Ch'i	chee
Qigong	Ch'i Kung	chee gung
Dao	Tao	dow
Dan Tian	Tan Tien	don tian
Wuji	Wu-chi	woo jee

Tai Chi will be an important part of global awakening.

~ Eckart Tolle

A BRIEF HISTORY

The Origins

It is believed that Taiji originated in 12th century China as a synthesis of martial arts exercise and sitting meditation. Its legendary founder, Chang San-feng, was a Daoist priest of the Sung dynasty. Inspired by a graceful crane and supple coiling snake in battle, Chang San-feng developed a system of self-defense based not on brute strength or physical force but on the power of flow and flexibility, yielding, rooting and returning energy. In addition to its martial arts benefits, Taiji was practiced as a holistic art with a focus on cultivating the healthy flow of Qi, the body's internal energy, designed to relax, develop and enhance the entire body.

A tradition of secrecy ardently guarded the Chinese internal and external martial arts. Held as a treasured secret, Taiji

Quan was passed down only to select members of successive generations – often within a single family. If and when Taiji was shared, it was primarily in the tangible, physical display of movement. Although fundamental to the practice, little information on its holistic emphasis of connecting body and mind was willingly shared. There is no doubt that these factors contributed to misunderstandings. Misconceptions intensified when Taiji began to take root in other parts of the world. With the complexity of the Chinese language lending itself to many translation interpretations, confusion was perpetuated thus limiting dissemination and growth. Only very recently has scientific research begun to open doors revealing the depth of this ancient art.

The Styles

Chen

Chang San-feng handed down his art to his disciple, Wang Chung-yueh, who wrote additional classics to preserve and promote the art. Gradually, Taiji moved to the Chen family who hid it from outsiders for over three centuries. Passed on from father to son, Taiji was practiced secretly by royalty in northern China. In the 1670s, Master Chen Wangting (1580-1660) developed the Chen style that is characterized by its explosive power, low stances and emphasis on spiral force. Similar to the martial arts, it contains movements that are hard and fast as well as slow and soft.

Yang *["young"]*

Master Yang Lu-Chan (1799-1872) became the first outsider allowed to study Taiji from the Chen family. After his training in the early 1800s, he returned to Beijing to teach Taiji to the royal family and to make it available to the general population for the purpose of maintaining fitness. It quickly became popular in martial arts circles. Later, he modified his style with higher stances and gentle, slow movements to make it more suitable for all ages seeking general good health and well-being. As a result, the Yang school was founded. However, it was Yang Lu-Chan's grandson, Yang Ch'eng-fu, who became the most dedicated and skillful Taiji master. In the early 20th century, he modified his family's form to be softer yet more internally powerful. Along with outstanding abilities, his kind nature drew many students to him. It was he who finalized the Yang style with its extended and graceful movements, making it the most famous and popular form in China today.

Wu and Wu/Hao

The Wu style originated with Wu Quanyou (1834-1902), who studied with Yang Lu-han. However, The Wu/Hoa style originated from Wu Yuxiang (1812-1880). He also studied with Yang Lu-Chan but he incorporated the small frame Chen style initially developing a lesser-known Wu style. This method was then passed on to Hao Weizheng (1849-1920), who made significant contributions to the lesser-known style, eventually creating the Wu/Hao style. Consequently, it is sometimes confusingly called the Hao style. Both creators studied the Yang and Chen forms in order to develop a unique style characterized by slow, agile, compact movements with an emphasis on correct body positioning.

Sun *["soong"]*

Sun Lu-tang (1861-1932), a well-known internal martial artist, created his own style by blending his expertise with that of both the Wu/Hao and Yang styles. The Sun style, often considered the most gentle, is characterized by an upright stance, supportive follow-steps and embedded Qigong, a system of special breathing exercises integrated with movement. Because of its gentleness, it is this style that is endorsed by arthritis foundations around the world.

Recent History

The Taiji styles of Chen, Yang and Wu emerged in the 19th century in China. Early in the 20th century, the Sun style was created. When Eastern philosophies first became popular in the Western world in the 1930s, Taiji was still zealously protected. It wasn't until 1964 that Cheng Man-Ch'ing, the famous student of Yang Ch'eng-fu, traveled to New York and was one of the first to teach Taiji openly to non-Chinese students. By the early 1970s, Taiji was taking root in the United States and Europe. Today, it is Cheng Man-Ch'ing's shortened and simplified version of the Yang style that has become one of the most popular forms worldwide.

Chinese Masters said,
"It doesn't matter the form. Follow the principles."

The DAO of TAIJI QUAN

For thousands of years, Chinese culture held a Daoist perspective, a philosophy that provided a path for living a simple life in harmony with the natural world where all elements are interconnected. This philosophy naturally influenced the development of Taiji Quan. The word *Taiji* is an ancient Daoist philosophical term symbolizing the interaction of yin and yang, which are opposite manifestations of the same forces in nature, a fluid never-ending relationship of energies.

Deeply rooted in traditional Chinese medicine, Taiji is often described as the mother of yin and yang, the regulator of the ever-shifting energies within the human body. Yin and yang create each other. The qualities of hardness and softness that each one represents overcome each other. The theory of yin/yang states that normal physiological activity of the human body results from unifying the opposites, coordinating the relationship between substance (yin) and function (yang). In physiological terms, the dynamic balance of yin and yang is homeostasis, the ability to maintain internal equilibrium conducive to life.

Yin / Yang

The symbol of yin and yang is a representation of all that exists in the body, in nature and in the world. The outer circle, representing unity, contains every existence within the same whole. All of our inner experience, such as emotions, and sensations, as well as those that are external, such as other people and the natural world, are all simply different expressions of the same whole.

The dark and light areas of the symbol indicate that within this unity, there is duality. Yin is inward, passive, receiving, soft, feminine and dark. Yang is outward, active, sending, hard, masculine and bright. In our world, we make identifications based on differences rather than sameness.

The small circles within the dark and light areas represent the idea that, although we perceive ourselves from the perspective of our separateness, there is nothing that is entirely separate from anything else.

The center of the symbol represents the balance point for all aspects of life. It is the still point where the inherent duality of the world unites and all apparent opposites unify.

The balanced interaction of yin and yang *is* Taiji and the overall attitude of the Taiji path is characterized by balance and moderation. This neutralization of extremes provides a way of looking at the world and traveling down a more tranquil existence within it. As we shift our perspective more to the center of any situation, we take a fundamental step in the cultivation of the Taiji mind. This balanced way, referred to in all the Buddha's teachings as the *middle path*, is a path of peace and essential to all Taiji practice.

THE POWER OF QI

Taiji Quan is meditation and movement that connects and exercises the mind and the body. It is the coordination of slow, graceful, fluid body movements that focus on the cultivation of internal energy, referred to as Qi, and designed to relax and nurture the entire body.

The concept of Qi has been a fundamental belief in Eastern cultures for thousands of years. Qi is the primordial energy that creates life and the power that flows through all living things. It is everything and everywhere. It is the vital life energy that comes from a combination of the air we breathe, the food we eat and the natural energy that we inherited at birth. It is the energy that sustains us during life and the energy that leaves us at death. Acupuncture and Chinese medicine base their central theory on the concept that good health relies on a full and vibrant supply of Qi, circulating throughout the body performing necessary functions.

Where The Qi Goes, The Blood Flows

It is understood that a healthy person has more Qi than one who is ill. However, good health is more than simply an abundance of Qi. Good health implies that the Qi within our physical form is vigorous, clear and free-flowing. Believed to reside in the blood, its healing energy is only helpful if it can flow to where it is needed, traveling through unique, intangible channels in the body called meridians. Meridians serve as an important map of our energetic body. Imagine an intricate electrical circuitry where energy courses throughout a physical being, carrying nourishment and providing pathways for communication between organs, the exterior and interior layers of the body, and the numerous networks within the system.

Chinese medical theory is based on the premise that poor health and disease result if Qi becomes imbalanced, stagnant or blocked. External factors such as trauma and internal factors such as stress contribute to this imbalance of energy. The Eastern view sees the body as a hologram where all aspects of its functional and energetic structure support each other and the physiological, emotional and spiritual components are intricately related.

The Dan Tian

The storage house of Qi is the Dan Tian, the center of the body. It is a small area situated three finger-breadths below the navel and located midway between the navel and the pubic bone. It is the body's center of energy, storing Qi like an energy reservoir and propelling the energy through the body like a pump. It is the body's core. It is the body's center of gravity.

Qigong

Qigong is the practice of cultivating Qi. It is essentially a breathing exercise aided by certain body movements and meditation at the same time. It is the discipline that focuses on nurturing the flow of life energy through dedicated practice. Often, it is asked if Qigong is a form of Taiji. Actually, it is just the opposite. Taiji is a form of Qigong where the whole body cultivates and encourages the free, unobstructed circulation of Qi. The rhythmic movement of the muscles, joints, and spine pump energy steadily throughout the body, opening up all the channels leading to good health and well-being. This idea of free circulation - Qi energy permeating all the inner workings of the entire body - is what the Chinese call *nourishing life*.

> *Directing the Qi is like threading a pearl*
> *with nine bends in its hole;*
> *there is nowhere it does not penetrate.*
>
> *~ Wang Zongyue*

THE TEN ESSENTIAL PRINCIPLES

The Ten Essential Principles of Taiji Quan are fundamental to all styles. Legendary Grandmaster Yang Ch'eng-fu, the father of modern Taiji and grandson of original Grandmaster Yang Lu-Chan (1799-1872), initially dictated the principles to Chen Weiming in 1925. Since then, they have become scripture to Taiji teachers and students worldwide.

Traditional Chinese Medicine takes a holistic approach that views the body as an integrated whole. In that approach, each of these principles relies on each other. If one is mastered, the others will follow, but if one is missing, the others will also fail. Many of these essential principles may appear obvious but it takes a dedicated, patient practitioner to fully understand and integrate them into the movements of the form. For the purpose of this work, rather than studying the ten principles in their original sequence, they are grouped into the three main categories of Mechanics, Movement and Mindfulness.

THE TEN ESSENTIAL PRINCIPLES

GRANDMASTER YANG CH'ENG-FU
Translation of the Original Chinese Text

1. Suspend the head and keep it straight
2. Depress the chest and raise the upper back
3. Loosen and straighten the waist
4. Distinguish between substantial and insubstantial
5. Sink the shoulders, drop the elbows, sit the wrist
6. Use your mind and not your force
7. Coordinate the upper and lower body movements
8. Unify internal and external movements
9. There must be absolute continuity of movement
10. Seek stillness in motion

The CARDINAL PRINCIPLE

RELAX

For hundreds of years, Chinese medical theory has taught that proper exercise and nutrition are major factors in good health. However, the most significant, underlying factor in good health is a calm, peaceful internal harmony. The very essence of Taiji Quan is to be completely relaxed and receptive. These qualities emerge out of a stillness that can only come from simply slowing down.

Unfortunately, our fast-paced lives have made us very uncomfortable with the absence of stimulation and speed. Our society is organized in such a way that even when we do have leisure time, we don't know how to use it to get in touch with ourselves. Phones, televisions and computers are just some of the countless ways we lose our precious time. We are uncomfortable with solitude. Instead of slowing down and reconnecting with ourselves, we too often try to escape from ourselves through more and more frenzied activity.

At first, the slow and quiet elements of Taiji Quan can be a little unnerving. However, to gain the art's benefits, slowing down is the first requirement. Taiji's slow movement brings awareness; a consciousness of what is subliminally happening within. It slows down our neurological speed and ushers us to deeper levels of being. By settling into a slow calmness, the mind can relax the body and the body, in turn, can relax the mind. Anxieties release, tensions untangle and the passageways of body and mind are allowed to open.

We strive for a clear mind and a body free from tension. With every part of the body relaxed, including every muscle and organ, the circulatory system extends and the resistance of vessels to blood is reduced. This happens throughout the practice as every part of the body is in motion. The circulation of blood becomes smooth. Every cell can gather adequate oxygen and nutrients while cell waste can be easily transported away. When doing Taiji, the homeostasis of the body is similar to a body at rest, but the improved circulation of blood is similar to that of the body in motion.

The entrance to Taiji's many levels begins with simply relaxing and letting go. Through relaxation, the blood is vitalized and the body's internal energy is cultivated deep into the sinews, tendons and connective tissue. The Qi is free to permeate the body and we are given a chance to release, to recharge, to heal.

> *Of all the principles of practice, the most significant foundational principle is that the mind and spirit should always be "xujing" described as "empty and tranquil". Xujing is the essence of Taiji – as well as the ultimate goal.*
>
> *~ Grandmaster Feng Zhiqiang*

MECHANICS

The first stage of concentration belongs to the body's structure. Correct postural alignment is one of the most important considerations in overall health and well-being, yet it is rarely a focus. In fact, many of us are unsure what a correct posture looks like. We often resort to our childhood training, believing that good posture means "standing to attention" - chest thrust out, belly sucked in, knees and hips locked creating an S-curve in the spine. Consequently, these misalignments and compressions of the spine create hunched, stressed shoulders, neck tensions, headaches and countless other ailments that compound over time.

As we advance in years, this structural misalignment becomes our reality. Joints wear, bones deform, energy drains. Rediscovering a correct alignment is not an easy task but the first step is simply awareness of each structural misalignment. Hopefully, with this awareness, we invite an acceptance and then pledge to take action to make the necessary corrections. Over time, this process of awareness, acceptance and action can foster positive changes, relieving debilitating symptoms and recreating a healthier body aligned with gravity and fueled from within.

Imagine the body as a set of building blocks stacked one on top of the other. The bottom block creates the solid foundation. If all the other blocks are placed to rest squarely on top of that foundation, the aligned blocks will result in a column of complete balance and stability. Take any of the blocks out of alignment and that balance is compromised. Correct alignment allows the body to stack all its building blocks, one on top of the other, for harmony with gravity. As an exercise that emphasizes the body's center of gravity, Taiji assists us in stabilizing ourselves.

The structure of the spine with its 24 vertebrae and its function - to provide the path of preserving life – is of utmost importance. As a practice of self-cultivation, classic Taiji masters viewed the spine as a strand of pearls ascending vertically. If allowed to lean, bend or collapse, the internal power and energy necessary to sustain the body would be lost. In Daoist physiology, the spine is "the Pillar of Heaven" with nerves and internal organs connected to it. If the spine is not correctly aligned and the internal organs are restricted, the energy of the body cannot flow freely. With a stable, aligned body, the bones and muscles begin to work together rather than in opposition; the joints and connective tissues are lubricated and stretched; the organs have the space they need to correctly function, and a more efficient use of oxygen leads to greater blood circulation.

You are only as young as your spine.
-Anonymous Ancient Chinese Saying

SUSPEND the HEAD and KEEP IT STRAIGHT

This is considered the most important of the ten essential principles. It is said that if the head is not properly aligned, the whole body will be out of alignment and the body's energy will be disrupted. Keeping the body erect and relaxed will facilitate proper circulation of Qi and blood, increasing flexibility in the whole body.

Yang Ch'eng-fu said, "Keep your head erect and do not incline it forward or backward, left nor right....But you should not hold it in a stiff manner." In practice, the position of the head must be strictly maintained, being held naturally erect as if a string is suspending its top.

- Allow the chin to tuck in slightly, releasing any tension in the back of the neck.

- Relax the muscles of the face. Relax the jaw, unclench the teeth. Let there be space in the mouth.

- Close the lips and rest the tongue on the palette above and behind the two front teeth, like saying the letter "L". The object of this is twofold. First, it gives us a reminder to soften this area. Secondly, in the science of acupuncture, it joins the 2 major meridians that run up the front and back of the body.

- Close the eyes. Soften the areas around the eye sockets and begin to focus inward.

- Move awareness to the crown of the head. Place the attention on the *baihui* [*"bye way"*] point, an important acupuncture point that corresponds to the soft spot on a baby's head. Be careful to visualize this point rather than the middle of the top of the skull, a common error. This causes the nose and chin to rise up creating pressure in the neck.

- Imagine that a strong silk string attached to this *baihui* point is suspending the body from above. Let the feeling of suspension decompress the area at the base of the neck and the feeling of spaciousness fill the areas between the vertebrae. Let the whole body hang with head and spine in perfect alignment.

- Rest the focus on this effortless, centered suspension. Relax.

- Breathe in and out evenly through the nose.

> *Make your spine upright as string of pearls that does not lean. But being tense, holding oneself unnaturally erect or overcorrecting are all real defects. You must know that these are dangerous. That is enough.*
> ~ Cheng Man-Ch'ing

Keeping the Head Straight
~ To Thine Own Self Be True

According to ancient Chinese thought, the universe – and all that exists within it - is a vast Oneness. There is no dependence or independence. There is only interdependence. Everything depends on everything else and that harmony is the basic principle of all existence. This Oneness is the *Dao*, an ever-evolving circle that is always moving in accordance with the laws of nature; change being its only constant. All Daoist philosophy emphasizes being attuned to these invisible laws of nature. Taiji is viewed as a way to connect with that deeper part of ourselves that knows what is best for us.

However, since we approach life with the rational mind, we see ourselves as separate from nature. Consequently, we think we can destroy nature without harming ourselves, or destroy our own nature in an effort to be something we are not. When we lose our feeling of Oneness, we acquire a sense of isolation and loneliness. In our modern society, we are given constant reminders that we are just not good enough. Along any street, we are offered ways to become more than what we already are. The most characteristic view of a Daoist belief is that everything already possesses the "buddha nature" so enlightenment is a matter of simply rediscovering that which we already are.

Taiji is a discipline, a practice that requires all one's being. It is an unending journey toward oneself and toward Oneness with all things. It is a way of life that demands an examination of self. At the same time, it demands total awareness of the world around the self. It is the art that connects us with the harmonious ebb and flow of our true nature and answers our quest for authenticity.

> *The snow goose need not bathe to make itself white. Neither need you do anything but be yourself.*
>
> ~ Lao Tzu

DEPRESS the CHEST and RAISE the UPPER BACK

This principle is the most often misinterpreted, leading to many errors in postural integrity. Simply defined, to depress the chest means to simply relax the chest muscles. Raising the upper back means to extend and lengthen the spine rather than have it hunch over. If the back is extended naturally, the chest will be neither concave nor convex.

Most people hold tension in the chest and ribcage due to bad posture, emotional patterns or poor breathing habits. Many people who try to relax the chest, tend to tilt the whole ribcage forward, creating a slouching posture. In the correction, rather than puffing out the chest, making the body top-heavy and creating an S-curve in the spine, relax the ribs so the front of the chest can drop down while the spine remains upright. Roll the shoulders back and down, shifting the shoulder blades closer together in the back. Without actually lifting the sternum, creating tension in the diaphragm and making abdominal breathing more difficult, simply imagine that the sternum is being gently lifted from above, opening the heart.

In Taiji, the spine is compared to a string of pearls. In a pearl necklace of value, the pearls are separated by tiny knots that act as spacers to protect the pearls from rubbing and scratching each other. In the human body, the spinal spacers are the spongy intervertebral discs that absorb shock and separate one bone from another. Each space within the spinal column is not only important for movement, it is essential for the life-sustaining action of the central nervous system.

Imagine the spine as a long string of pearls and the tailbone as a pendulum anchoring that string. Gently tilt the tailbone toward the earth and focus on lengthening the spine. Open up the spaces between each of the vertebrae. This is the key to loosening the lumbar section of the vertebral column and aligning the head and body. With proper alignment achieved, the vertebral column straightens and its movable joints relax. Spinal curves are reduced and resiliency is encouraged.

Proper alignment in conjunction with relaxation of the ribs encourages correct breathing, allowing the inhalation to expand the lower lungs and waist rather than chest breathing which is typically shallow and inefficient. As the long, full breath oxygenates the body, it immediately engages the relaxation response, bypassing the brain and sending messages of calm straight into the nervous system. The body relaxes; the heart beats more slowly and regularly; the mind quiets.

In Taiji, correct breathing fuels the body and is a vital aspect of every movement. It is the basis of gathering, storing and delivering energy. When we inhale, we gather and accumulate energy. When we exhale, we deliver energy. Think of bellows in a continual process of drawing and delivering oxygen to bring life to a waning fire. At each inhalation, think of filling the body with life-energy. At each exhalation, think of releasing tensions. Think of the continual, natural rotation of in and out with neither effort nor force.

Qigong is the exercise of gathering, accumulating and transforming energy. Every Taiji practice, if performed correctly, is a beautiful, flowing Qigong exercise. In correct breathing, called abdominal, diaphragmatic, or *Dan Tian* breathing, the lower abdomen moves out with inhalation and in with exhalation. During inhalation, the diaphragm drops, pushing the abdomen out as the lungs expand and fill with air. During exhalation, the diaphragm relaxes and moves back up, the abdomen gently contracts, forcing air out. Healthy diaphragmatic breathing gently massages the digestive organs while it continuously strengthens the abdominal muscles and all of the muscles involved in respiration.

For practice, first, take time to connect with the breath. Then, mentally follow the free flow of each breath into the belly, following each expansion with a gentle release of any tension. More specifically, visualize the free movement of Qi reaching, then leaving, the area of the lower abdomen. Focus on the natural sound of the breath ebbing and flowing like the waves along the shore. Remember, there should be nothing forced or strained. There is simply gentle awareness.

- Stand in correct postural alignment. Feet should be shoulder-width apart; knees bent, not locked.

- Focus on Essential Principle #1. Be suspended. Imagine being lifted upward from an imaginary string at the *baihui* point, the acupuncture point that corresponds to the soft spot on a baby's head. Tuck the chin in slightly, releasing any tension in the back of the neck.

- Soften the face. Rest the tongue on the palate behind the two front teeth. Relax.

- Roll the shoulders back and down and let the shoulder blades melt down the spine.

- Relax the chest muscles. Imagine the sternum being lifted and the heart allowed to open.

- Tuck the tailbone in slightly. Think of it as a pendulum gently pointing downward to the earth, anchoring the spine.

- Mentally scan upwards through the spinal column, visualizing the spine as the 'long string of pearls'. See each of the vertebrae as a single pearl surrounded by space. Take extra care around the base of the skull, where the spinal cord exits the brain. Relax and soften this area that is so often compressed with tension.

- Breathe in and out through the nose. Each breath is long and slow. Breathe in and feel the spaces open, elongating the spine. Breathe out and observe a gentle closing, encouraging a relaxed, neutral spine.

- Shift the awareness of the breath into the belly and out of the belly. Let the abdomen expand and contract. Each inhalation fills the belly with new energy; each exhalation releases tension.

- Keep the natural, relaxed flow of the diaphragmatic breath until it no longer feels comfortable. Then resume normal breathing.

Most important is to relax. Let go of your tensions and hard, stiff force. Open up all the passageways in your body to the flow of the Qi.

-Cheng Man-ch'ing

Putting Your Back Into It
~ Patience and Perseverance

Taiji teaches us to relax. It provides calm in our chaos and balance in our lives. Yet for all it promises to deliver, Taiji requires that practitioners give it a little loyalty in exchange - loyalty defined as patience and perseverance. These are the qualities needed to create a firm foundation for the practice of Taiji. A firm foundation then provides assurance of better health and well-being.

In Taiji, as in life, the importance of patience and perseverance cannot be overstated. Patience is about taking the time needed to get a movement right, all the while understanding that getting it right is not a crucial matter. Perseverance is about making the time and effort to practice regularly, knowing that while benefits come with each practice, it is a lifelong learning. Taiji requires discipline and consistency but with no set goals, instant gratification, belts or certificates, many students lose interest and lack the motivation to continue. Taiji is a lifetime study. Those who do continue with practice, discover its depth and many treasures. Practice, governed by patience and perseverance, connects and transforms the body, mind and soul. Gradually, Taiji becomes a way of life.

It takes courage to be patient and slow down in a world constantly threatened by the rushed thoughts and actions of today's fast pace. Taiji's slow, controlled movements counterbalance the world's disquiet and give us some time to connect with our inner selves; to soften and reevaluate reactions. The tenets of patience and perseverance cement an allegiance to Taiji. Both build character and strengthen the mind. In time, they help define who we are and how we relate to the world.

> *Taiji is equal measures of quality*
> *of movement and perseverance.*
> *If a man plants melons, he will reap melons;*
> *If he sows beans, he will reap beans.*
>
> ~Old Chinese Proverb

LOOSEN and STRAIGHTEN the WAIST

In Taiji, the waist is considered to be the area below the ribs and above the pelvis including the hips. It is also considered the biggest and most powerful "joint" in the body. Consisting of complex core muscles that act together as the steering wheel for the entire body, the waist is central to all Taiji movement. The Chinese classics say that with a loosened, relaxed waist, the breath is allowed to move freely, the energy can be directed quickly, the extremities will work together, and balance will be stable. Yang Ch'eng-fu called this area "the kingpin of the body".

The concept of *loosening* is rather misleading. The emphasis is not on relaxing the waist but working towards a strong, flexible one. Taiji's fluidity and ultimate power come from movement that originates from the central, largest muscles at the core of the body, before translating outward to the smaller muscles of the extremities. Learning this act of 'loosening' can take some effort. The key is to focus on the most important area called the Dan Tian, the Daoist term that refers to the body's center of energy. Located three finger-breadths (1.3 inches) below the navel, 3/4 of the way back to front, it is where Qi, the energy of the body, is gathered, nurtured and stored. The Dan Tian both stores Qi, like an energy reservoir, and propels Qi through the body, like a pump, opening and activating the channels of the body to ensure vibrant health. In physiology, it is referred to as the body's center of gravity. Focusing on the Dan Tian bolsters the internal strength and vigor of the whole body, reinforcing posture to encourage flexibility and the integration of movement.

- Place the feet parallel to each other and hip-width apart; the outer side of the foot should create a straight edge.

- Make suction cups out of the toes to lift the arches of the feet and gently open the hip joints outward.

- Place awareness on the "Bubbling Well" foot point, one-third the distance from the base of the second toe to the back of the heel, for sensing balance and establishing a connection with the earth.

- Gently tuck in the tailbone. Allow it to drop downward so that the tip is directed towards the earth rather than tipped at an angle. Doing this, the top of the head and the tip of the tailbone should be in the same vertical line. Maintaining this posture elongates and relaxes the spine. In movement, it develops agility in turning the body.

- Imagine that the pelvic area is a bowl filled with water kept at a neutral level – not tilted towards the front or the back. Take care that the stomach muscles are not floppy or sagging but pulled firmly inwards and upwards helping to stabilize and support the spine.

- Connect with the breath. Mentally follow the free flow of the diaphragmatic breath reaching the lower lungs. With each expansion, let it be filled with the energy of life, followed by a gentle dispersing of this energy throughout the entire body.

- Focus on lowering or sinking this energy, the Qi, to the Dan Tian on the exhalation. To sink the Qi is to *will* the Qi to accumulate in the Dan Tian. Focus on the *intention* of gathering and nurturing energy there. If this is difficult to do, simply concentrate on the physical location of the Dan Tian and think of energy gathering there.

- With each breath, imagine the Dan Tian filling with energy and then spilling that energy through the channels of the body, renewing and recharging as it courses throughout the body.

- Think of that area of the waist as the *brains* in control to navigate and direct movement. With a flexible core, an energetic connection within the body is awakened.

The ancient masters said,
"At all times, pay attention to the waist.
The lumbar region is the axis.
Heed the lumbar section every minute."

Loosening the Waist
~ Getting to the Core of the Matter

Taiji is a grounding and centering exercise designed to integrate the body and mind to find balance. As a scale balances weight, Taiji begins with centering on the core of the body, the center of gravity, to equalize energies. Its goal is to nurture these internal energies through practice and achieve the balanced interactions of yin and yang.

In Taiji, as in life, balance – of both physical and mental properties - is key. While Taiji integrates mind and body, it also helps integrate the skeletal and muscular systems. Moving through each slow step, breathing deepens and muscles relax. Flexibility, balance and coordination is increased; the immune system is strengthened; and the body's natural healing powers are enhanced. Moving through each slow step, the mind becomes calm. The right and left brain hemispheres connect as they need to for clearer thinking and mental focus is improved. Studies indicate that just by doing a few simple movements, we can unblock the body's energies, freeing them to flow in a pattern conducive to learning, and enter the creative state of mind known as the alpha state.

Taiji clears the communication between mind and body. Through practice, we learn to slow down, to take time, and to trust our own intuition. Knowing that skill in Taiji cannot be reached if the inner nature is out of balance, we work to nurture, replenish, and balance the yin and yang energies in ourselves to improve our form. As practice deepens, the interrelationship of the physical, mental and spiritual becomes apparent and our form becomes an external manifestation of our inner spirit. Through these efforts, it doesn't take long before we notice an improvement in ourselves that reaches into and enriches our daily lives.

Through dedicated practice, we are taught the importance of keeping balance of strength and grace in a world unnerved by haste. The smoothness of each movement reflects how we travel through each day and through the changes of our lives. With a balanced, nurtured, inner spirit, we can extend an element of calm to each interpersonal relationship. It is through this connection that we can promote peace.

The body should be supple like an infant;
The movements should be flexible like a snake;
The feeling should be soft like water;
The breathing should be smooth like a cloud.

~ Old Chinese Proverb

SINK the SHOULDERS, DROP the ELBOWS, SIT the WRIST

The shoulders have a tendency to harbor most of the body's tensions. One of the most difficult things for most beginning Taiji practitioners is to relax this area. Often, we are completely unaware of the tensions we develop and carry there. To "Sink the Shoulders" means they should be neither shrugged nor collapsed. If the shoulders are tensed, the power of the arms will be isolated, stopping the delivery of strength. The shoulders and elbows, while capable of a wide range of motion, have only a small range where they function well and are in harmony with the stabilizing muscles and connective tissue of the body's central core. To "Drop the Elbows" means that they should be neither raised nor squeezed. Releasing tension in the upper body lets the shoulders and the elbows behave naturally and they will automatically sink.

- To loosen and sink the shoulders, roll them back and downward as low as they can go in their natural position.

- Be careful to keep the spine erect - not slouching forward.

- Imagine the sternum being lifted by an imaginary string. Feel the heart opening as the shoulder blades are gently drawn close together in the back.

- To drop the elbows, move them toward the ground. Imagine that there are weights hanging from the tips of the elbows pulling them down, making them heavy. Special awareness needs to go to the elbows to maintain this heaviness and secure the correct sinking of the shoulders. If the elbows rise up tension is created in the shoulder.

To "Sit the Wrist" means that the hand is relaxed and in line with the arm. This is traditionally called "beautiful lady's hand" with fingers neither closed nor open; neither bent nor straight. Place intentions on relaxing all the ligaments in the hand right to the tips of the finger. If the ligaments can relax, blood circulation will improve. Often, there is an increased sensation of warmth at the fingertips as the Qi moves freely. No force is used. From relaxed softness alone, progress happens.

- To sit the wrist, relax the hand with the fingers forming a gentle curve. Imagine holding a large ball. Imagine softness.

- Focus on Qi moving from the Dan Tian, traveling freely to the palm, and then dispersing to the tips of the fingers. If the hand or fingers are too bent or rigid, energy is blocked.

Sinking the Shoulders
~ Carrying the Weight of the World

Lifestyle, diet and emotional pressures all affect the flow of energy in the body on a daily basis. Poor posture and habitually awkward positions or tensions can actually weaken the energy channels. Injury to the organs, tissues, bones or muscles through which these channels flow upsets natural internal harmony, inhibiting the energy flow.

The repetitive strain of our daily routine places great demands on our health. For those who must work slumped over a desk or keyboard, energy deficiency in the chest weakens the lungs, making them susceptible to common respiratory conditions. For those who must stand for long periods of time, energy congestion develops pain or problems in the hips, back and kidneys.

Correct alignment of the body is essential for the smooth flow of Qi energy. Postural alignment is the fundamental principle for practice. We must first, however, know what correct postural alignment is before we can recognize repetitive strain and understand how misalignments encourage bad habits that will result in discomfort.

Taiji is all about awareness. Once we know how the body *should* be aligned, we can begin to correct a lifetime of bad habits. Begin by increasing the awareness of what is really going on in your body. Try to relax enough to discover where the body cannot relax. Seek out the tensions of the day and focus awareness there. Visualize the tightness melting away with each breath. Enjoy a quality of relaxation deep within that can only be experienced by the awareness given to it. Know that – for all its promise and potential – Taiji's benefits will only accumulate if the movements themselves express this precise quality of relaxation and calm.

In Taiji, we take the awareness within. Soon, the awareness expands outward. As we focus on the gentle release of tensions and tightness deep within the body, we extend that focus to other tensions created in relationships and interactions that inhibit or damage our connectedness with others. By letting our view of a centered self release, we are able to give way to a broader sense of the world where beliefs are relative. There, we can attempt acceptance and understanding. Perhaps then, we can vow to amend.

Tension is who you think you should be.
Relaxation is who you are.

~Ancient Chinese Proverb

MOVEMENT

With the first essential principles, the body learns how to be balanced and aligned. This becomes the posture of Wuji, the stance that gives us the strong, stable foundation required for movement. In Wuji, there is the sense of being rooted deep below the earth with our foundation stabilized. At the same, there is a sense of being held from above with our foundation suspended. As we separate from Wuji and prepare for movement, Taiji is born.

Taiji combines postural integrity and relaxation with movement that emerges from the stillness of rooted feet, bringing ground strength up through the legs. The slow, steady weight shifting begins between the yin and yang forces of our nature. This energy is then directed by the waist, up through the torso to the shoulders and then sent out through the hands. Kinesthetically, it is similar to dominos falling consecutively. Once movement begins, a chain of action is triggered. As each individual piece is affected, it, in turn, affects another. The steady, continuous pattern of energy moves through the entire structure until completion.

Like a great river, Taiji movement continually flows and steadily follows the same principles that keep the universe pulsing with energies. Free the body of any tension so that its energies can travel freely through it. Let the mind command this energy flow. Let the internal vigor stream smoothly through each movement to increase the generation of strength. Give awareness to the calm within each slow, steady continuous motion.

> *The root is in the feet; energy issues up through the legs, is controlled by the waist, and expressed in the hands and fingers.*
>
> *- Chang San-feng*

DISTINGUISH BETWEEN SUBSTANTIAL and INSUBSTANTIAL

Mobility and the generation of power come from the awareness of shifting the body's weight. Being able to differentiate between what is substantial and insubstantial or what is full/heavy and empty/light translates into agility in each movement. Clear distinction between the leg that is the supporting leg and the leg that is empty of weight is the first step towards smooth coordination of each movement and the development of balance. The key to the change of substantial and insubstantial is the understanding of weight transference, the ability to transfer strength from one leg to the other.

Weight-Shifting Exercise

- Shift all the weight to one leg while maintaining an upright posture. This becomes the full/heavy, substantial supporting leg.

- When this leg becomes completely full/heavy and capable of supporting the body's weight, pick up the other empty/light, insubstantial foot. Take a step; touch down gently.

- Gradually, as more weight is placed onto the insubstantial foot, slowly and consciously transfer the rest of the weight. Feel the weight shifting, filling up the leg again like sand pouring into a vessel. Feel the body stabilize.

- Repeat the process to develop awareness.

Visualizing each movement before actually moving will help distinguish the substantial and the insubstantial. Be mindful of each step of the process. First, be aware of the heaviness on one side of the body. Feel the whole body's weight resting on only one leg. Firmly plant the heavy leg first; then prepare for movement. Move like a cat. Move as though walking on ice, unsure of support, or walking in the dark, unsure of footing. Practicing the transference of weight from one leg to the other will improve mobility, coordination, stability and balance.

The Taiji Walk

With the head the size and weight of a bowling ball supported by a spine that leans, for many people, walking becomes more of a controlled falling, with the upper body leading and equilibrium compromised. Taiji walking is the basis for *rooting*, *grounding* and *weight shifting* skills that are fundamental requirements in every Taiji form. They are also essential skills that support us in our daily lives. With an upright posture and the deliberate shifting of weight from one foot to the other, we learn to move from our center of gravity, the Dan Tian.

In Taiji Walking, often taught as a fall prevention exercise, the eyes should look straight ahead, the mind should be focused on the bottom of the feet, and breathing should be normal. All movements and weight shifting are done as slowly as possible, building strength, balance and endurance.

The ultimate goal is to be so aligned with gravity and have such control of movement that if someone said *"Stop!"*, could it be done? Could the challenge of stopping mid-movement be met with a balanced, centered and rooted body?

- Place both feet together, weight evenly distributed, with the knees slightly bent.
- Place all the body's weight onto one leg, which then becomes the substantial, full leg.

- Slowly lift up the foot of the other leg, which is now insubstantial and empty of weight. Slowly take a natural step forward. Shorter steps are easier. Place the heel down first, the toes pointing forward. Slowly place the rest of the foot onto the floor, but no weight should be on this foot yet. Concentrate on the sensation of the floor beneath the body.

- As slowly as possible, transfer weight onto the front foot until there is no weight on the back empty foot. With the heels of both feet on the floor, the back foot and leg is now empty/insubstantial and the front foot and leg full/substantial.

- As slowly as possible shift the weight from the front foot to the back foot, until all the weight is on the back foot.

- With all the weight on the back full/substantial foot, slightly lift the toes of the front foot and turn it on its heel until the toes point outward about 45 degrees.

- Place the whole of the front foot on the floor and slowly transfer all the weight to the turned-out front foot.

- Slowly pick up the back foot, move it towards the front foot and then take a natural step forward. Place the heel on the floor first and then the rest of the foot, with the whole front foot now pointing forward.

- Repeat the sequence.

Distinguish Between Full and Empty
~ Defining Priorities

We do not always have the luxury of choosing which activities go into our daily routine. We do, however, always have the choice of how we go about them all. How we stand and sit; pull and push; bend and lift all contribute to overall well-being. Once there is an awareness of how inner harmony is manifested, it is our responsibility to make choices that will encourage harmony rather than deplete the energies that contribute to it.

So just how do we move throughout the day - traveling smoothly with a sense of purpose or stumbling blindly on the whims of the wind? The ability to differentiate between what is substantial and insubstantial in our lives is what allows us to prioritize. Determining the importance of one thought or action over another assists in creating a focus in movement throughout our day. Clear distinction between what is full and what is empty establishes a roadmap for life. It is the ability to distinguish between what gives us joy and what robs our energies; what provides richness in life and what holds no value.

It is the goal of Taiji to have a clear mind and a body free of tension. The ability to differentiate between the substantial and insubstantial translates into agility in movement but also in our approach to life. Once we know how to recognize what makes our lives full, we can begin to shift our focus to what contributes to a healthy body, mind and spirit; to what gives us a sense of purpose to make every day count. Once we are able to differentiate, we can detach ourselves from whatever depletes us. We can choose to avoid negative thoughts, actions, emotions and individuals. Instead, we can redirect our intentions toward positive influences. We can allow those positive dynamics to untangle tensions and worries, open channels of awareness and communication and restore internal harmony.

> *Watch your thoughts; they become words.*
> *Watch your words; they become actions.*
> *Watch your actions; they become habit.*
> *Watch your habits; they become character.*
> *Watch your character; it becomes your destiny.*
>
> *~ Lao Tzu*

COORDINATE the UPPER and LOWER BODY MOVEMENTS

Taiji entails a constant interaction between the upper and lower body. With this interaction, the whole body performs as one integrated unit. When the arms move, the legs should move with them. The hands and feet, the elbows and knees, the shoulders and hips should all move in concert. All the body's joints should feel that they are connected, with each part of the body threaded together and moving in harmony.

The Taiji classics say, "Motion should be rooted in the feet, released through the legs, controlled by the waist, and manifested by the hands through the shoulders and arms." In other words, when the feet and waist move, the shifting of weight should occur with the arms and hands following and contributing to the flow of energy. This coordinated path is achieved by first making sure that the feet are always firmly rooted to the ground like the roots of a tree. The knees must remain slightly flexed. Finally, the upper and lower body must move harmoniously so that all parts of the body are strung together without the slightest break. Even the focus of the eyes moves accordingly.

The understanding of this principle is subtle, but its essence is that the whole body moves in a coordinated stream of movement uniting the upper and lower body. When one part moves, everything moves. When one part is still, everything is still. A common instance of uncoordinated movement is when the arm has completed the move before the leg and the arm must wait for the leg to catch up before it can perform the next movement. The upper and lower body must be in time with each other. Whenever they are not synchronized, coordination is lost. Whenever there is lack of coordination, Taiji movement will lack strength and appear disjointed.

Visualizing the head, torso and pelvis as a single column assists in creating coordinated movement. With the spine erect, consider the upper body as a cylinder aligned over the stable base of legs and feet. All arm movements are initiated by the upright rotation of this column or cylinder. Focus on the center of this cylinder and let it control the movement. Be a cylinder and move from this center.

Taking this one step further, try the imagery exercise below. This helps us understand that when we act as a cylinder, we are moving from our center of gravity, the Dan Tian, and allowing it to act as one central hub, connecting and coordinating all upper and lower movement. It is this that creates the image of the effortless flow of motion characteristic of Taiji.

Imagery Exercise:

- Stand in Wuji - feet rooted, knees soft, shoulders back, spine erect and aligned, head suspended.

- In preparation for movement, visualize the hipbones as headlamps that send out parallel beams of light that illuminate the landscape in front of the body.

- Shifting the body's weight to one leg, notice the body turns slightly. As the body shifts to one side, the beams of the headlamps turn also, remaining parallel, horizontal and pointing in the direction of travel.

- Continue with the opposite leg. Feel the weight shift turn the body. Visualize the parallel beams of light.

- Repeat the sequence.

As soon as you move, your entire body should be light and sensitive and all its parts connected. All the joints of the body should be connected without permitting the slightest break.

- Chang San-feng

Coordinate the Upper and Lower
~ Harmonizing

Taiji's goal is to nurture internal energies and achieve balanced interactions of the yin and yang forces within us. Through dedicated practice, we learn to neutralize emotional tensions and excesses that influence and affect interpersonal relationships.

One of the most important keys in life is to discover how to feel connected with others and maintain harmonious relationships. It is unfortunate that much of the world's discord is fueled by a basic unwillingness to accept differences or the inability to manage those differences.

Two major players in most unharmonious relationships are criticism and blame. Both block our ability to take a clear look at any given situation. When we blame others for the problems in our lives, we become passive victims of circumstances. When we criticize others, we become focused on negativity. When faults capture our attention, respect is lost. If we are to take responsibility for our problems, we first must be willing to look at ourselves objectively and seek to change the only thing we can change – ourselves. It is a common belief that when we change our attitude or perspective, the world also seems to change. In terms of relationships, taking personal responsibility for problems and shifting perspective can often release tensions that damage our connectedness with others.

Our minds are powerful, creative mechanisms. Our thoughts and beliefs become perspectives of our reality. The judgments of good and bad or better and worse depend on our awareness of it. The very essence of Taiji Quan is to be receptive to both the yin and yang aspects of life and to be aware of what is going on in the present moment. Awareness is being in touch with both yin and yang aspects of life. Under the influence of awareness, we become more attentive and accepting. This is the gateway to restoring harmony.

Life is filled with conflicts, but it can also be filled with calm if we are willing to connect with it. Through acceptance of ourselves and others, within the power of the present moment, resolve or change can emerge, accompanied by a willingness to appreciate the fact that harmony is always available to us to restore richness in life.

*Our attitude towards life
determines life's attitude towards us.*

~ Lao Tzu

THERE MUST BE ABSOLUTE CONTINUITY of MOVEMENT

Taiji is fluid. Its movement is a constant ebb and flow alternating between soft and hard, empty and full, yin and yang, and the gathering and delivering of energy. Based on principles of Daoism, the art of Taiji lets us experience the very laws of nature in our own being. Like the world turning and the river flowing, Taiji movement is slow, steady and continuous. This is a more difficult task than it appears. It takes great skill to move continuously in perfect consort with mind, body and breath.

Just as our breath is continuous, so are our movements. They are circular, revolving without interruption, without limitation, from beginning to end. The classics refer to the continuous nature of Taiji movements as a great rolling river and that the circulation of the inner strength resembles the unraveling of silk from a cocoon.

Think of the circular path of each movement. In Taiji, every movement is in a curve or circle that has no beginning or ending. As one movement of the form is completed, another seamlessly begins. In practice, movements are slow and continuous, never speeding up, never slowing down. These slow, steady continuous movements against gentle resistance improve flexibility, balance, stability and strength.

Try to maintain the same slow, smooth, controlled speed throughout the entire form. Imagine being in water with its gentle resistance influencing every motion. Feel the soft resistance on the outside of the body and the controlled flow of movement on the inside of the body. Use the image of the reeling silk thread from a cocoon. Reeling silk from a cocoon requires a steady hand. If, at any point, the speed or strength of the pull is varied, the silk will be damaged. Reeling too quickly will break the silk while reeling too slowly will tangle it. In Taiji, train with the mindset of one steady, uninterrupted, continuous pull of motion.

Be still as a mountain,
Move like a great river.

~ Wu Yuxing

Continuous Motion Exercise:

- Stand in Wuji - feet rooted, knees soft, shoulders back, spine aligned, head suspended.

- Raise the writing hand to shoulder-height and write a word or name in the air with each large cursive letter flowing into the next one.

- Focus on its continuous, circular path moving smoothly and steadily without interruption.

- Move the arms as though they are moving through thick honey or molasses. Feel each movement as strength against a gentle resistance.

- Try it with the other hand.

- Try it with attention given to the breath, joining it to movement. Let this simple exercise become a Qigong practice.

Continuity of Movement
- Slow and Steady Wins

The path of a novice practitioner begins with the choreography of a Taiji style. Along the way, the essential principles are integrated and we begin to learn how to relax tensions from the body, release impatience from the mind, and recognize the Qi energy within us. Somewhere in the early stages of this journey, a common question arises: *"When do I get there?"*

Most people require a destination and, preferably, a timeframe for getting there. With Taiji, however, there is neither destination nor timeframe. The uncomfortable fact is - we never get there. The real achievement of Taiji is an intrinsic reward, one that gives a sense of personal fulfillment. To varying degrees, it becomes a way of life that perpetuates itself.

Sun Lu-Tang, the creator of the Sun style and one of the greatest Taiji masters in history, believed that the highest level of Taiji is not to become invincible in skill, but is at understanding the Dao, one's nature. In other words, Taiji students only become proficient and skillful when there is harmony and balance within themselves and within their connection to the surrounding environment.

Although it may seem complicated, actually it is all very simple. In Taiji practice, as in life, we just do one thing at a time. The focus becomes *letting go* - releasing unnecessary worries and tensions and removing negative thoughts and emotions. We pay attention to nurturing the body and spirit with breath and mindfulness. Our intention is balance and harmony, not perfection. We learn that by taking care of the present, with every thought and every action, we are also cultivating and protecting our future.

Somehow, moving steadily along this path, progress takes care of itself. We recognize a comfort that comes from our involvement with a deeper self. The gifts of practice are revealed. Life is simplified. Soon, there is the realization of just how unimportant a destination is. Taiji is a life's journey. It is a gradual, endless process of awareness, nurturing, conditioning and improvement. It is a path of peace, guiding our way in a very confusing world - one slow, steady step at a time.

*A good traveler has no fixed plans,
and is not intent on arriving.*

- Lao Tzu

MINDFULNESS

The various forms of Taiji, despite having different styles and characteristics, all have the same training principles. The whole body is relaxed with emphasis placed on inner rather than outer force. Emphasis on exertion of the mind rather than the muscles provides a valuable training method for strengthening health and raising the level of the art. In Taiji, the aim is serenity in movement; to integrate mind and body.

The mind has a powerful effect on the body. Taiji integrates the two. The conscious mind directs an internal force and the internal force directs each movement. The ancient masters believed that inner energy translated to outward power. This inner energy, called *internal vigor*, is completely different from the force of the skeletal muscles. To master the art, differentiating between this internal vigor and muscular force is necessary.

When practicing Taiji, it is important to focus on all the movements and the coordination of the holistic body. During practice, the mind needs to be steady and with one-pointed concentration. This mindfulness, however, goes beyond an intent focus on what is happening. The quality of perception also plays an important role. With perception, we keep present and absorbed. Mindfulness, through its strong power of keen awareness and observation, involves an internal energy and the ability to uncover our own characteristic nature. In Taiji, power and strength come from the mind. Our health is a reflection of our state of mind. Our mind is the root of who we are.

Power comes from within.
Let the mind lead the energy to lead the strength.

-Ancient masters of Taiji Quan

USE YOUR MIND
NOT YOUR FORCE

In Taiji, the focus is on the internal rather than external. The aim is to develop the coordination of mind, energy and strength. Where muscular exercises improve physical power, Taiji practice strengthens the internal workings, placing no value on muscular strength. Internal strength is developed by relaxing the muscles and loosening all the joints as fully as possible rather than using the force of the skeletal muscles. The ancient Daoist masters believed that in order to maintain strength and vitality of youth, the body's internal energies - organs, glands and all the systems - had to be vibrant. Exercise and diet are important for general well-being, but if the internal energies are not working in a balanced way, energy and strength are lost and dis-ease is inevitable.

This essential principle centers on strength and energy coming from within and being directed by the mind. But if muscular strength isn't used, where does Taiji strength come from? Master Yang Ban-hou, second generation direct line from the Yang style founder, told Wu Quan-you, the founder of the Wu style, that the secret of Taiji's internal vigor comes from the body's sinew, the ligaments and tendons which constitute the body's connective tissue. Relaxing and loosening all the sinew, joints and muscles as fully as possible rather than using the force of the skeletal muscles develops internal strength.

In Chinese philosophy, the practice of relaxing and loosening these internal components is called '*song*'. It is a difficult concept for most of us to grasp but it is a cornerstone in every form of Taiji. The translation doesn't reveal its complexity, which involves consciously and gently stretching the joints from within and mentally focusing on expanding the joints internally. When the joints are loosened, the body's sinews and connective tissues are exercised and allowed to stretch open. Channels within the body are then conducive for the free flow of energy to support strength.

American anatomist, James E. Crouch wrote: "the functions of connective tissues are as varied as the tissues themselves. Binding, supporting and protecting are the most obvious and purely mechanical ones. But they are also involved in the vital concerns of circulation of body fluids and storage of excess food materials. Some of them play an essential role in inflammation." Therefore, exercising the sinews is very important for health and longevity.

> *When you are extremely soft,*
> *You become extremely strong.*
>
> *-Ancient masters of Taiji Quan*

The experienced master of Taiji Quan is very accomplished at '*song*' to gather internal strength but also in what is called '*ting jing*' or *listening energy*, the ability to move the body through the use of the body's proprioceptive sense. The body's proprioceptors -sensory receptors found in muscles, tendons, joints and the inner ear – are designed to detect motion and position of the body in gravity. Their responsibility is to provide stability and increase sensitivity in relation to balance. Encouraging the mind to tune into the body's proprioceptors develops *listening energy*. Mentally focusing on expanding from within relaxes internal workings and releases muscular tensions. Through these systems of *song* and *ting jing*, the mind leads the internal energy for strength within each movement and lets our internal channels open for power.

Keep the mind fully and intentionally engaged along each and every tiny point along the path of the movement and each point of the body. The mind directs the movements. The body simply follows.

Using The Body/Mind In Practice

- Stand in Wuji. Free the mind of any outside thoughts or distractions.

- Be present. Stay mindful of the power of being centered in this moment.

- Use the mind to loosen and relax all the connective workings of the body. With the mind's eye, see the spaces of the joints expanding; feel the spaces around the bones and cartilage becoming open and lubricated.

- Use the mind to scan for any tensions the body is holding. Observe any tightness. Gently stretch and mentally expand the muscles and tissues of that area. Breath in space and openness.

- Relax the spine. Imagine the spine as a long string of pearls held together on an elastic thread that runs from the back of the neck to the tailbone. Imagine that this elastic thread is gently stretched from both ends, so that the base of the skull floats upwards as the tailbone moves downward. Feel gently stretched from both ends. Visualize the string lengthening and allowing more space between each of the pearls. Now, shift the awareness to the spine opening and allowing more space between each vertebra, remaining loose and flexible even as it lengthens.

- Bend the knees and stretch the hip joints gently outwards creating an arch. Sink down with the tailbone pointing to the earth. Feel a gentle expansion within. Imagine sitting on a high chair or barstool. Feel supported.

- Loosen the elbows, wrists and finger joints. Stretch them out as if gently pulling the joint open. As the joints are gently stretched this way, the practice of *song* comes in, improving flexibility, building internal strength, and opening the internal channels to the flow of Qi energy.

- Tune in to the proprioceptive sense aligning the body with gravity. Focus on the "Bubbling Well" foot point, one-third the distance from the base of the second toe to the back of the heel, for sensing balance and establishing a connection with the earth.

- When beginning the form, practice with a mental focus on the inherent nature and execution of each slow, steady movement.

- Keep the intention on the power of being centered. Use the mind to open and direct the flow of energy.

- As long as the focus is on each slow, steady motion, awareness and mindfulness will increase. Every tiny movement will grow internal calm.

What is the main principle of Taiji Quan?
The mind is the primary actor
and the body the secondary one.

-Ancient masters of Taiji Quan

Use Your Mind Not Your Force
~ Be Strong

No matter how in control of our circumstances we feel, life can test and challenge us. Life is movement filled with unforeseen circumstances. Some circumstances, we can control, but those beyond our control meet us with resistance and negative force.

Much of our struggle to be content arises when we stubbornly resist what is going on in our lives. Often, we resist facing life as it is because that would mean abandoning our views of how we think it *should* be. Resistance is the ego's effort to maintain control. Unfortunately, the more we continue a struggle with resistance, the tighter its stronghold becomes. Sooner or later, we must decide between determined opposition or reluctant acceptance. Either we continue our struggle which often results in frustration and disappointment or we forfeit control and accept. With acceptance, rigidity softens. We can bend with the harsh winds of challenge and renew our trust in the laws of nature. Like a big willow, strength is the surrendering to that which we cannot conquer.

According to Chinese medicine, internal strength creates external power. The paradox is that the more relaxed the body is, the stronger it can become. Taiji's strength comes from its softness within the supple, smooth flow of each movement like a natural, free-flowing river meandering to the sea, its current unchallenged. As it pumps energy throughout the body, it improves circulation, increases the assimilation of nutrients and prevents muscle breakdown caused by tensions and stress. As it trains the mind to focus, intention uses whatever strength is available and directs it efficiently. It teaches us how to focus integrated power; posture, body and breath all working together.

Strangely enough, when we learn to surrender to our reality, stop resisting and accept a situation, there is suddenly a relief, a physical and mental release of tension, and an opening of the mind and spirit. With acceptance, we can let go of today's struggle and let in compassion that initiates the creative process of change. When we begin to accept, we can relax and experience a change in our own energy pattern. Then, we are able to tap into the positive energy available to us and feel a renewed sense of direction, courage and strength.

Returning is the motion of the Dao.
Yielding is the way of the Dao.

~ *The Tao Te Ching*

UNIFY INTERNAL and EXTERNAL MOVEMENTS

Taiji requires an understanding of the strong relationship between thought/emotion and posture/movement. The mind, as commander of the body, has a profound influence on the workings of the body. With concentration and mindfulness in practice, the body and mind are harmonized and there is no division between what the mind directs and the instantaneous response in the body.

Taiji trains the spirit. The Taiji classics say, "The spirit is the master and the body is its servant. If you can lift your spirit, your movements will become light and nimble". The nature of all movement consists of substantial (hard, solid) and insubstantial (soft, empty); expansion (opening) and contraction (closing). This applies not only to the external workings of movement, posture and body but also to the internal workings of the mind, inner force, and spirit. Postures are nothing more than solid and empty. Opening and closing not only concerns the hands and feet, but the hands and feet must work in concordance with the opening and closing of the heart/spirit and mind as well. With focus and intention, the mind and spirit unite with the external movement. When the internal and external are synchronized, the body can move as one complete integrated unit without interruption.

It is this principle in particular that qualifies Taiji Quan as an internal martial art. With its great emphasis on mind/body unity, the most important factor is the use of '*jengjing*', using whole body power in one complete, integrated entity. Power is generated with the body as a singular unit and energy is generated from this unified power source.

The Daoists realized that a relaxed body controlled by a quiet mind produced a holistic entity, capable of fulfilling its potential. At the earliest stages of training, Taiji focuses on refining and training the nervous system to control the body. Through mind/body unity, we seek to balance the nervous and hormonal systems, thereby producing a power from within the body. The unified power is completely dependent upon fine neuromuscular control, which is completely directed by the mind.

Most Taiji forms are practiced slowly. A fundamental reason for this is to allow for constant monitoring and adjusting of the body to make sure it is moving as a unit. It is much easier to feel moving slowly than quickly. Eventually, the body will develop into a strong, supple unit that allows the frame to act as a spring against the ground. This type of power is impossible unless the body is always maintained in a unit, just as a spring is one continuous thread of steel.

Achieving and maintaining the unified relationship of internal and external is a difficult process. The most significant component of this interaction is the breath. With breath, the nerves, blood vessels, muscles, ligaments and tissue release tension. With breath, vital energy flows in the wake of the mind or consciousness and circulates all over the body. With breath, the internal and external connect and Qi is cultivated.

> *In practicing Taiji, don't move the hands by themselves. If you move the hands, it is not Taiji. Taiji Quan is Taiji Quan because the external and the internal become unified as one.*
>
> *~ Master Chien-hou*

Using The Body/Breath In Practice

To inhale fully and exhale completely in a controlled manner is like a baby's breathing, the correct, natural way of breathing that we have forgotten over time. Watch a sleeping baby. The whole body inhales and the whole body exhales. When we breathe this way, the breath slows, blood is filled with life-giving oxygen, and respiration becomes more efficient - all bringing a feeling of relaxation and calm.

- Imagine a balloon in the lower abdomen located about 3-5 inches below the navel and inward, hidden inside.

- With the inward breath, imagine that the inhaled air goes straight down to the balloon. With the exhalation, imagine that the balloon collapses. Let the mind watch the breath move in and out of the body.

- Be aware of the body at this moment. Practice 3 or 4 more breaths. Practicing breathing this way for only a few minutes every day, cultivates Qi, the personal intrinsic energy that gives so many gifts of well-being.

- Let each new breath be slow, deep and smooth just as the sea's tides ebb and flow.

- Follow the wave of each breath as it enters the body, fills the belly, then permeates the physical form before it exits to begin the journey again and again. Follow the wave of each breath as it washes over and relaxes the entire body.

- Imagine each cell within the bones, organs, muscles and ligaments being infused with the rich fullness of each inhalation, filling it with renewed life.

- With each exhalation, release the toxins of the mind and body and let them go.

- Follow the breath. Let the breath lead the way. Be completely immersed in the tranquil flowing energy.

In time, it may be helpful to watch the breath in Taiji practice, incorporating breath with movement. As the form begins, simply watch the breath. Nothing is forced or uncomfortable. With a regular, dedicated, practice of the form - fueled by the focus of the breath - the ability to harmonize these systems will improve. View each practice as a path towards growth and be content with each small step towards this goal. Remember that the reward of practicing Taiji is in the *process* of getting there. Progression is what matters, not the destination – and always keep in mind that no one reaches perfection.

The spirit is like a concealed sword.
From the outside, your practice has the appearance
of being relaxed and comfortable
But on the inside, your spirit is concentrated and
sharp as a sword.

-Ancient masters of Taiji Quan

Unify Internal and External
~ Be Present

The ebb and flow of life is like the sea. Sometimes, it is calm and peaceful but other times it is so loud that it threatens to overpower us. Sometimes, we struggle against being swept away by strong waves of difficult emotions or pulled by an undercurrent of conflict. By keeping this truth in mind while skillfully living in the present moment, it is possible to develop a more balanced approach and therefore experience a greater sense of equanimity in life.

Time is an illusion. We know that the past is gone and the future has yet to be realized. However, we also know that the thoughts and actions of today will pave our path and will be reflected in the future that lies ahead. The one thing that will put us in good stead is a consciousness of each present moment. When we are fully present, our inner eye brings awareness and we are able to get in touch with our very nature. Rather than going through life in a fog of oblivion, we are able to see where we are within the ebb and flow of life. We can navigate through the challenges that are presented to us and accept what each challenge may offer.

Being present means staying right here, right now, with intention – being as we are, where we are – and it begins with the breath. By simply drawing in a slow, deep breath through the nose and releasing it through the nose, we engage a relaxation response. When we breathe through the mouth, the reverse is true. It triggers a subtle anxiety response, which increases heart rate and redirects blood flow.

The act of being present is a meditation. It is the mindfulness of the breath that connects our inner self with the universal harmony. With each inhalation, we acknowledge the power of the present moment. With each exhalation, we release the burdens of the past and the anxieties of the future. It becomes a simple yet profound cycle that can change the way we perceive the world.

Taiji, like all practices that help us connect with our inner selves, is a powerful tool for waking us up and bringing us into the present moment. It helps us slow down long enough to recognize negative patterns and opens us to new, more positive possibilities.

> *Breathing in, I calm body and mind.*
> *Breathing out, I smile.*
> *Dwelling in the present moment, I know*
> *this is the only moment.*
>
> *~ Thich Nhat Hanh*

SEEK STILLNESS IN MOTION

Seeking calm within movement is a primary characteristic that differentiates Taiji from any other physical exercise, where stress is often placed on the body. Taiji's soft and gentle, slow and relaxed movements invigorate the body while they simultaneously offer the mind the benefits of rest. When practicing Taiji, we open ourselves to an awareness of inner workings and create a sense of tranquility. From this serene perspective, like being centered in the eye of a hurricane, stillness within movement is possible.

However, the stillness sought goes beyond a simple sense of ease. In Chinese philosophy, this stillness is a serenity, a mental quietness called '*jing*'. It is the stillness that holds great energy in total harmony. It is the calm that harmonizes yin and yang, the life forces of the nature within us where there is no ego, no fear, no anger. When we seek stillness in motion, we ask for a meditative mind.

Many who have unsuccessfully sought tranquility in seated meditation have turned to Taiji. For those, the flowing, slowly unfolding form is far more suitable for meditation than sitting motionless and struggling to control the monkey mind with mental imaging, mantra or breath. Through full attention to each movement, our focus grows towards an introspective mind where our thoughts are not constantly jumping from past events to hoped-for or feared events in the future. Our focus is centered on the present action of 'letting go' and savoring the moment of simply *being*, instead diluting it with worries about the past or fears of the future.

Taiji, as a meditative art, lets us uncoil from our everyday lives of enervating responsibilities and obligations, transporting us into quiet and calm where equilibrium can be found. It helps us transition from our everyday life to a space that is the very nucleus of our being, the center of self that is sacred. Here, the energy that has been stripped away during our day has a way to replenish and the process of gathering and centering our energy can begin to recharge us.

We all have this sacred center of ultimate peace; but attaining any degree of serenity takes time. It is difficult for the mind to release itself from the spin of whirling thoughts. At first, it is just easier to let our monkey-minds jump randomly from branch to branch. Yet each time there is an attempt to go deeper within, to dive deeper than the superficial splashes on the surface, there is the opportunity to find a moment of mental quietness and a feeling of returning to our own home within; to our very essence, a place where we are truly and naturally ourselves.

> *Like the dragon diving*
> *into the depths of the ocean,*
> *Or the snow leopard returning*
> *to the mountain forests.*
>
> *~Ancient Chinese Proverb*

With each practice, our return is welcomed and we stay a little longer. Soon, the monkey-mind doesn't interfere so often with the mindfulness within each movement. After a while, the quietness found carries over into the rest of the day and helps us approach concerns with a new perspective. Somehow problems are reduced in proportion and we are no longer completely at the mercy of overactive imaginations and heightened perceptions. As practice grows, it becomes easier to transition from an everyday existence to that space where scattered energies can settle into a *jing* state of mind, where we open, receive and renew.

The quieter you become,
The more you can hear.
~ Ram Das

Using The Body/Spirit In Practice

- In Wuji, think of quietness from within.

- Imagine a peaceful environment like a tranquil rainforest or a placid lake.

- Relax here. Set aside the everyday constructed self.

- Slowly begin the form, bring focus to the body's actions.

- Maintain the intention of being present

- Let each slow, steady continuous movement become a wave of energy

- Let each ebb and flow harmonize with gentle breath. With each breath, the mind is calmed.

The quiet comes into contact with the movement,
Then the movement simulates the quiet.

-Ancient masters of Taiji Quan

Seek Stillness
~ Be Centered

We all have a deep-seated desire for comfort and a life free of anxiety. Somehow, we carry a belief that if we try long and hard enough, we will be rewarded with happiness and a stress-free existence. Often, when this is not forthcoming, we become disillusioned and begin to believe that there must be something wrong with *us*.

Judgments are based on ideals and expectations, strengthened by beliefs and illusions removed from reality. As we move closer to our own true nature, we understand that the essence of practice is the ability to center the body, mind and spirit. In this experience, we can honestly acknowledge whatever is happening in regard to the present moment. There are no demands to feel or be anything other than an authentic observer. We can disengage from illusion, judgment, and our relationship with past and future. In this way, we can be involved with a true appreciation for life just as it is.

Taiji's focus on the coordination of slow movement and breath quiets the spirit and reminds us of our connection to life. As we feel the breath and sense the body, we expand our awareness of the vital energy that enters and surrounds us. As we still the mind, we find harmony with life and, with that, an understanding that we *are* vital energies within a vast universe. As we settle into our center, we open our hearts and place trust in a universe that nourishes and supports us. With trust, we are humbled. With trust, we can experience the freedom of being at one with the natural flow of the universe and give birth to serenity of the soul.

> *Who can make the muddy water clear?*
> *Let it be still, and it will gradually become clear.*
> *Who can secure the condition of rest?*
> *Let movement go on,*
> *and the condition of rest will gradually arise.*
>
> ~ *The Tao Te Ching*

THE DEVELOPMENT OF PRACTICE

The best way to improve one's Taiji is to devote more time practicing it.

~ Master Jou, Tsung Hwa

As we stand in preparation for Taiji movement, we seek quiet. We spend time to release tensions and distractions, to slow everything down, to relax and experience a quiet state of internal harmony. This is Wuji, the position of primal energy. In Chinese philosophy, Wuji is understood as complete nothingness. It is absolute quiet, void of any movement. It is the quiet that settles us at the very beginning and rewards us after the very end. Taiji comes from Wuji and returns to it.

Wuji allows us to create a solid foundation for practice. When our foundation or *root* is stable and strong, our body is also stable and strong like a well-rooted tree. With a strong foundation, our body will perform well and our practice will develop.

THE SILENT STRENGTH OF WUJI

Before Taiji, it is Wuji. It was in a state of mixed Qi.
Thus, Wuji is called the Mother of Taiji,
  the power before myriad things were created.

~ Grand Master Mr. Tu-Nan Wu

RELAX

Bring attention into the awareness of the body. Be present and mindful. Stand naturally with the feet placed shoulder-width apart. Place the hands to the side with the palms facing inwardly and relax the whole body. Close the eyes and feel the skin and the muscles supporting them; mentally check for tension and encourage full relaxation there. Move down to the angles of the jaw making sure the teeth are not clenched. Let the tongue lightly touch the roof of the mouth behind the two front teeth. Then let the sense of relaxation travel down the sides of the neck. Tuck in the chin slightly and feel a gentle release in the back of the neck. Exhale to let the chest relax. Take the mind to the right shoulder; let it sink down; feel as if weights are attached to the elbows and the right hand is hanging heavily by the side of the body. Then go over to the left shoulder and let it sink down as well. Gently roll the shoulders back and down, bringing the shoulder blades closer together in the back and the heart lifting in the front. Imagine that a soothing stream of clear water is washing down the back, carrying any obstructions away with it. Feel the downward movement pass through the body, relaxing every muscle. Feel the weight sinking down through the legs to the soles of the feet. Focus on the "Bubbling Well" foot point connecting and rooting the body to the earth.

ALIGN

Keep body upright: head erect, back straight, shoulders back, down and aligned over the hips, the knees slightly bent and the tailbone gently tucked in like a pendulum pointing to the earth. Now, take the awareness to the *bai hui* [*"bye way"*] point, the soft 'baby spot' at the top of the head. Imagine that the head is being suspended from a fine silver string and let the body hang gently and effortlessly. Feel the spine lengthen and decompress. Stand still in this position with the body correctly aligned between the ground and the sky, poised between heaven and earth. Sense the drawing of Qi energy from the two great forces of heaven and earth.

Imagine cleansing the whole body from the inside. Sense warm water slowly trickling down from above, starting at the top of the head, moving through the body, and exiting from the bottom of the feet, releasing any remaining tensions.

In this shape, seek equality by emptying and releasing various parts of the body. Start by checking for any tension in the right side of the body, then go to the left. Equalize them by releasing any tensions that are found. Move to the upper and lower hemispheres of the body. Check and equalize. Check the front and back aspects of the body followed by the inner and outer aspects. Aim for the release of any tension in order to be balanced and equal. Release what can be released, accept what cannot. Tensions often give way with practice.

Much of the process is initiated by the mind, but as time goes on, it is worth releasing the control of the mind and opening trust in the body and spirit. After dedicated practice and training, muscle memory and body/mind awareness naturally gravitate to correct form and its ability to release tensions.

BREATHE

Breathe naturally through the nose. Relax the diaphragm so that it expands with each inhalation and contracts with each exhalation. Keep everything relaxed. Gently steer attention to the lower abdomen, the Dan Tian. Keep the focus there as long as it feels comfortable then return to a natural breath. Maintain a slow, relaxed breathing pattern. Think of the breath as a long string of energy as it enters the nostrils, moves down to the belly, circling, energizing and harmonizing before it takes its route back up and out.

Place gentle awareness on rooted standing, breathing and body awareness. Nothing is uncomfortable or forced. Relax. Experience calm. Within this framework, a heightened awareness grants ability to sense a pulse throughout various junctures of the body and utilizes the breath to enhance the flow of Qi throughout, permeating the organs to increase functionality. Prepare to combine mental focus and physical action.

Inhale to bring you strength
Exhale to give you freedom.

-Anonymous Taiji Saying

THE MINDFUL MOVEMENT OF TAIJI

Let your body become as strong as an oak
and as flexible as a willow;
Let your mind become as clear as still water.
This is the essence of Taiji Quan.

-Ancient masters of Taiji Quan

AWARENESS

After the fundamental foundation of Wuji, we are prepared for Taiji and guided to movement. As we initiate body to form, the principles of *Mechanics* and *Movement* are incorporated. Focus on the slow, relaxed, continuous movement; put the mind in each precise shift. Imagine moving in water and feel its gentle resistance. Nothing can be done quickly. Feel the gentle swell of the water surrounding and supporting the body as it shifts forward and back. Let the body move with the wave-like flow and feel the strength within it. Focus on strength, not strain. Shift the awareness to an internal strength that fills each movement with buoyancy that comes from a mental awareness rather than the use of the muscle. Within this framework, a heightened awareness allows the ability to sense a pulse throughout various junctures of the body. It utilizes the breath to enhance the flow of Qi throughout, permeating the organs to increase functionality. Let the form become a flow of nature. Unite mental focus and physical action. Achieve a state of relaxed inner calm while in motion.

CULTIVATION

Taiji is an exercise of the mind. The mind directs energy. The movement of energy is the movement of Taiji. The ten essential principles assist in the development of smooth, flowing movements and a calm, tranquil mind. Devoting constant and regular attention to practice will refine Taiji skills and the energy that is generated. Through a dedicated practice, the qualities of any form will be enriched.

> *Work with diligence and care*
> *and the light in you will grow.*
>
> *-Ancient masters of Taiji Quan*

Do the form three times in succession. Practice first for the bones, muscles, tissues and all the internal workings; second for the mind; third for the spirit.

- First – Go through the form simply to refresh the memory. Relax.

- Second – Go through the form paying particular attention to technique. Put emphasis on one of the Essential Principles. Release.

- Third – Flow through the form. Be involved with the pure pleasure of relaxing and releasing. Renew.

When the form is complete, return to Wuji. Rest here. Be still. Discover Oneness.

> Taiji Quan first mobilizes, then leads to movement. One uses the mind to mobilize the Qi energy and then uses Qi to move the body. This movement extends from the inside outward to the external. It originates in the internal organs and then is conveyed outward through the movements of the arms and legs. This is the process of sinking the Qi to the Dan Tian. In short, one becomes supple through being light and agile. One must not use even the slightest force. Cultivate the Qi and circulate the blood. Stretch your ligaments and conserve your energy. When you practice Taiji Quan in the morning or evening, you only need seven minutes. It is especially important not to seek progress too soon.
>
> ~ Cheng Man-Ch'ing

CLOSING

Taiji is a comprehensive physical, mental and spiritual discipline. Its objective to restore the free flow of Qi within the body fosters our ability to manage stress and synchronize the ever-changing, yin/yang systems of life. It offers us a way to be fully present in the here and now, to be fully aware and mindful of this very moment and open to the magnificence of our pure existence.

The Essential Principles of Taiji Quan aims to deliver pathways that will lead to a body in harmony within a world of discord. Regardless of the form, if we are steadfast in the understanding and practice of the principles, we are promised health improvement, a meaningful change in our quality of life and the gift of our true essence to the world.

Learn Taiji exactly as you are taught;
Your true nature will polish it off effortlessly.

-Anonymous Ancient Taiji Saying

Allow yourself to yield, and
You can stay centered.

Allow yourself to bend, and
You will stay straight.

Allow yourself to empty, and
You will be filled.

Allow yourself to tire, and
You will be renewed.

The Tao Te Ching

RESOURCES

Cheng, Man-ch'ing. *Cheng-Tzu's Thirteen Treatises on T'ai Chi Ch'uan.* Berkeley, California: Blue Snake Books, 1985.

Chopra, Deepak, M.D. *Ageless Body, Timeless Mind: The Quantum Alternative to Growing Old.* New York: Crown Publishers, 1993.

Chuckrow, Robert, Ph.D. *A Clarification of "Secret" Teachings Revealed By Cheng Man-Ch'ing.* Temecula, CA.: *Qi* Magazine, Journal of Traditional Eastern Health & Fitness, Winter 2010.

Chuen, Master Lam Kam. *Tai Chi: The Natural Way to Strength and Health.* New York: Simon and Schuster Inc., 1994.

Cohen, Kenneth. *The Way of Qigong: The Art and Science of Chinese Energy Healing.* New York: Ballantine Books, 1997.

Douglas, Bill. *The Complete Idiot's Guide to T'ai Chi & Qigong.* New York: Penguin Books, 2005.

Da, Liu. *T'ai Chi Ch'uan and Meditation.* New York: Schocken Books, Inc., 1986.

Das, Lama Surya. *Awakening the Buddha Within.* New York: Bantam Publishing, 1997.

Davis, Deborah. *Women's Qigong for Health & Longevity.* Boston, Mass.: Shambhala Publications, Inc., 2008.

Emerson, Margaret. *Taiji Principles and Concepts.* Temecula, CA.: *Qi* Magazine, Journal of Traditional Eastern Health & Fitness, Autumn 2009.

Frantzis, Bruce. *T'ai Chi Health For Life.* New York: Wiley Publishing, Inc., 2001.

Jou, Tsung Hwa. *The Dao of TaijiQuan: Way to Rejuvenation.* Scottsdale, AZ.: Tai Chi Foundation, 2001.

Krauz, Herman. *The Tai Chi Handbook, Exercise, Meditation and Self-Defense.* New York: The Overlook Press, 2009.

Lam, Paul, M.D. *Yang Cheng-Fu's Ten Essential Points.* Temecula, CA.: *Qi* Magazine, Journal of Traditional Eastern Health & Fitness, Autumn 1999.

Lash, John. *The Spirit of Tai Chi.* London, England: Vega Publishing, 2002.

Lei, Qu Lei. *The Simple Art of Tai Chi.* New York: Sterling Publishing Co., 2004.

Liang, T.T. *Venerable Taiji Master.* Interview. Temecula, CA.: Qi Magazine, Journal of Traditional Eastern Health & Fitness, Spring 1993.

Lowenthal, Wolfe. *There Are No Secrets: Professor Cheng Man Ch'ing and His T'ai Chi Chuan.* New York: North Atlantic Books, 1993.

Mellish, Martin. *A Tai Chi Imagery Workbook - Spirit, Intent and Motion.* London, England: Singing Dragon Publishers, 2011.

Montaigue, Erle. *The Old Yang Style TaijiQuan.* Murwillumbah, NSW, Australia: Moontagu Books, 2000.

Nhat, Hahn, Thich. *Thich Nhat Hanh: Essential Writings.* New York: Orbis Books, 2001.

Olson, Stuart, trans., *The Intrinsic Energies of T'ai Chi Ch'uan*, St. Paul, MN: Dragon Door Publication, 1994.

Rones, Ramel. *Sunrise Tai Chi, Simplified Tai Chi for Health & Longevity.* Boston, Mass.: YMAA Publication Center, 2007.

Sharp, Gerald. *Where Precision Meets Simplicity.* Temecula, CA.: *Qi* Magazine, Journal of Traditional Eastern Health & Fitness, Autumn 2011.

Talbot, Rob. *Breathing for TaijiQuan: A Dissertation Concerning Natural Breathing Methods and Their Appropriate Use in Taiji and Qigong.* Qi Magazine, Autumn/Winter 2011.

Walker, Brian Brown. *The Tao Te Ching of Lao Tzu /* translation. New York: St. Martin' Press, 1995.

Yang, Yang, Ph.D. *TaijiQuan: The Art of Nurturing, The Science of Power.* Champaign, Illinois: Zhenwu Publications, 2005.

Yu, Tricia. *Tai Chi Mind and Body.* New York: DK Publishing, 2003.

ABOUT THE AUTHOR

Nancy Deye has spent much of her life in the practice and study of Yoga and Taiji Quan disciplines. She holds a Master's degree in Education and is a certified instructor of the Sun and Yang styles of Taiji Quan. Currently, she teaches in the Traverse City, Michigan area, where she lives and works on her other passion, silversmithing and lapidary work.

Made in the USA
Middletown, DE
05 September 2017